dogs & clouds & love & life

by

Sheila & Ron Stewart

dogs & clouds & love & life

Copyright © 1998

by Sheila & Ron Stewart

All rights reserved.
Unauthorized reproduction, in
whole or in part, is prohibited.

Printed in U.S.A.

ISBN: 0-9656856-5-9

Published by
Acadia Scale Press

Books by Sheila & Ron Stewart

500 All Time Funniest Golf Jokes, Stories & Fairway Wisdom

500 All Time Funniest Jokes & Stories About Gambling

500 All Time Funniest Jokes & Stories About Sex

500 More All Time Funniest Golf Jokes, Stories & Fairway Wisdom

Another 500 All Time Funniest Golf Jokes, Stories & Fairway Wisdom

500 All Time Funniest *Slightly Off The Fairway* Golf Jokes, Stories & Fairway Wisdom

Dogs & Clouds & Love & Life

The Professor Murders

The Sandstorm Connection

For Cole

dogs & clouds & love & life

UPS AND DOWNS

Life has many ups and downs,
Some times more downs than ups.
Forget the days that have the downs,
Enjoy the days with ups.

Sheila & Ron Stewart

Clouds take on many different shapes and sizes and characteristics. Sometimes they are welcome, sometimes they are ominous, and sometimes they are just there to study and enjoy. Clouds can be just about anything we want them to be.

CLOUDS

Sometimes the clouds beneath the wing
Are drifts of Arctic snow,
Sometimes a field of gray and blue,
Stretched out for miles below.
Sometimes in fog they drift around
And cover up the sun,
And bring a cold and eerie
Apprehension when they come.
Sometimes they hang like puffs of smoke,
Or pillows in the air,
Or waves upon a sea of mist,
Or whitecaps everywhere.
Sometimes the clouds are black with rain,
Or gray as dusk appears,
Their edges flamed with red and orange
As daylight disappears.
And sometimes when the clouds are gone,
Their images remain,
As shadows on the distant earth,
Five miles below the plane.

Diets are a little bit like clouds. They can be just about anything we want them to be.

THE DIET

I started on the diet
With a lightly buttered roll,
Followed by a donut
With a weight reducing hole.

There was nothing to it,
Losing weight was fun,
I ate a piece of low cal pie,
Then had another one.

It only takes a little will
To help us lose the weight,
To prove my will, I only ate
Three quarters of a cake.

We don't have to eat food
Just because it's there,
I ate a dish of cookies
But not because they were.

A body needs nutrition
And so I ate some bread,
And without a five course meal,
Why, I'd be underfed.

It's just a case of knowing
When we've had enough,
For someone who can't do it,
A diet must be tough.

Have you ever read a scary book or watched a horror movie, and then gone to bed and pulled the blankets up tight around your chin, as though they would somehow protect you from the evil creatures and villains that are lurking in your imagination.

SLEEP

I lay awake and wonder why
No sleep will come to tired eyes,
And ask myself what could it be
That's keeping peaceful sleep from me.

Could it be the onion dip,
The crackers, cheese, potato chips,
The pizza pie that I was fed
Just before I came to bed.

No.

That could never be enough
To make my dozing off so tough.

The horror movie that I watched,
The blood and guts and green stuff splotched
Across the late night T.V. screen
Surely could have never been
Enough to keep me wide awake
All huddled up for safety sake
Beneath the covers all secured
In fear that 'thing' somehow endured.

I read a book on murderers
And psychopaths and other curs,
And check the doors and search the walls
And watch each shadow as it crawls
On spider's webs and cracks until
The sun glints on my window sill.

By now my upset stomach's gone,
The 'thing' left with first light of dawn,
The murder in the book I read
Is finished now, the villain's dead.

My heavy eyelids slowly close
As peaceful sleep begins to flow,
And in my dreams I wonder why
No sleep would come to tired eyes.

Sheila & Ron Stewart

We remember lots of roads, but none is more familiar or welcome than the one we travel on our way home.

ROADS

They pass river banks,
And shores of lakes,
And mountain sides,
And ocean tides.

They cross fertile lands,
And desert sands,
And grassy plains,
And forest lanes.

They pass wealthy homes,
And poor folks zones,
And urban towns,
And parks and downs.

But of them all,
The road best known,
Is still the one
That takes us home.

Many of us resist using a calculator because we are afraid we might lose some of the mathematical abilities it has taken us so long to learn.

But, like everyone else, we eventually succumb. It is just so much easier adding up all those numbers with a machine than actually thinking.

THE CALCULATOR

The calculator helps us
With all we need to know,
It does our thinking for us
With its numbers all aglow.

But when it breaks we panic,
We don't know what to do,
How do we know for certain
That one plus one is two.

The calculator told us,
And we knew it must be right,
It gave us all the answers
As it blinked its little lights.

Our work must stop until its fixed,
To think would take too long,
And without the calculator
Our answers might be wrong.

We'll just wait 'till it returns
And tells us what to do,
We don't want to take a chance
That one plus one's not two.

"DOGS" was written for Tara, a loveable, feisty and arrogant, schnauzer sheepdog mix, whose company we enjoyed for eighteen years. We can't remember Tara ever doing anything on terms other than her own. She did not belong to us, we belonged to her. Come to think about it, she was very much like all our other dogs.

DOGS

Come, I gestured to the dog,
Come here, I ordered, come.
My finger pointed to the spot
I wanted her to come.

The dog lay there upon the lawn,
No movement could I see,
Except an eyebrow that she raised
To steal a glance at me.

Come, I ordered one more time,
This time she raised her head,
Then turned and looked the other way,
Ignoring what I said.

Come, you dumb animal,
I gave her one more chance,
To come when she was ordered to,
I took a threatening stance.

I whistled and I jerked my thumb,
You'd better come, I screamed,
She lay her head upon her paws,
The dog was deaf it seemed.

Please come, I changed my tone of voice
To soften my commands,
Perhaps if I were nice, she would
Give in to my demands.

She perked an ear and glanced my way,
She rose from where she lay,
She wagged her tail and scratched a flea,
Then turned and walked away.

I chased her all around the yard,
I grabbed her by the neck,
Come, I hissed between my teeth,
This time you'll come, by heck.

I dragged her to the spot
Where I had ordered her to come,
Then stroked the mangy cur and said,
Nice doggie, you have come.

Now heel, I snapped releasing her,
I knew now she'd obey.
No sooner did I speak the words,
Again she ran away.

Once more I chased her 'round the yard,
I dragged and ordered, heel,

She snarled and braced her stubborn feet
Against this new ordeal.

Heel, heel, I pointed to my side,
Damn you heel, I swore,
She smiled a stupid doggish smile,
And ran away once more.

Don't heel, don't come, I bared my teeth,
I roared, my face was red,
She didn't come or heel, she did
Exactly what I said.

She sat, I growled at her to sit,
I snarled for her to lay,
She made no sign of getting up,
I barked a threatening stay.

Soon she'll want her evening meal,
She'll woof for me to come,
And as I fetch, I'll wonder,
Which of us is dumb.

She will sleep and bury bones,
As dogs are meant to do,
And unaware, she'll sometimes do
What I have asked her to.

Sheila & Ron Stewart

Sunrises are often the most beautiful time of the day, and we miss too many of them.

DAWN

**Remnants of the night still lie,
As shades of purple climb the sky,
And slowly change to mauve and blue,
And orange and then a yellow hue.**

**Each new color swells and spreads,
And scatters crimsons, wines, and reds,
That glow until with darkness gone,
The rising sun completes the dawn.**

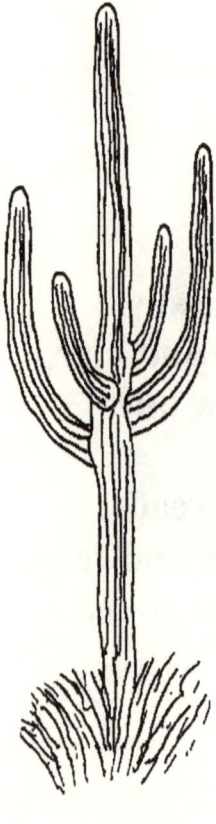

There are many different kinds of cactus in the Southwestern United States.
The most popular is the Saguaro. Pronounced su-ware-oh.

THE CACTUS

The cactus grows in burning sands,
Its branches arcked like giant hands,
Escaping from the searing heat,
While all around in still defeat,
The desert plants and grasses lie,
Parched and lifeless, brown and dry.

The cactus lives where nature gives
The cruelest that it has to give,
Where merciless through cloudless skies,
On barren earth baked hard and dry,
The sun beats down and sets aflame
Emotions that cry out for rain.

At last the night winds gently blow
Across the sunset's yellow glow,
The evening shadows slowly creep
And wake the creatures from their sleep,
And in the darkness all around
The cactus, desert life abounds.

All through the night the desert lives
As nature gives what it can give,
Then coolness of the night is gone,
And in its place the heat of dawn,
Sweeps across and burns the sands,
Where all alone the cactus stands.

Picacho Peak is one of those small mountain ranges that seems closer than it actually is. It appears on the horizon soon after leaving Phoenix on the way to Tucson and takes an hour to arrive.

The only civil war battle fought in Arizona occurred at Picacho Peak. Most people drive by without knowing the battle ever took place.

PICACHO

The peaks of Picacho rise above
The bones of soldiers lost in love
Of causes that they fought in vain
Where they could never hope to gain
A victory even if they won
The battle in the desert sun.

The war is heard in silent sounds
And felt across the battle grounds
Where wasted ghosts that no one seeks
Cry out in silence from the peaks
And wonder why nobody cares
Or even knows that they are there.

Cairn O'Mount rises and falls in Scotland, near Aberdeen, between the towns of Banchory and Brechin.

CAIRN O'MOUNT

Cairn O'Mount to local blokes,
And guides and other friendly folks,
Is just a wee small hill to climb,
An easy trip to save them time.

You'll cut off eighteen miles they'll say,
Then chuckle as you drive away,
For Cairn O'Mount is long and mean,
With roads few civil men have seen.

At first you'll pass through level downs,
And friendly fields and sleepy towns,
Designed in such a way to sooth
Your fears on landscapes flat and smooth.

But soon the road will coil and rise,
And disappear into the skies,
Then plummet down a sixteen grade
Some ancient cruel surveyor made.

For fourteen miles you'll heave and drop,
And pray the bloody road will stop,
And let you somehow reach your goal,
And save your uncourageous soul.

And when at last your drive is done,
You'll share your fears with local sons,
And hear disdainful laughter ring,
And see the mirth your story brings.

For they don't see a danger there,
Or share the fear you've had to bear,
For them it's just a wee small climb,
An easy trip to save them time.

Some villages stay small. Most do not. They grow into larger towns and then are swallowed up by even larger cities, and after a while we have difficulty recognizing that they have ever been there.

GROWTH

Once a tiny village lay
Among the fields of wheat and hay,
And shady trees and shining streams,
And quiet roads and simple dreams.

As time went by the village grew
Into a town that spread all through
The flattened fields and filled in streams
And chopped down trees and ruined dreams.

A city grew upon the town,
The village had been torn down,

The city's progress didn't care
About the lives of people there.

In time a mighty city lay
Between the walls of cement and clay,
And steel and glass and bricks and beams,
And planners' complicated schemes.

The mighty city was replaced
By larger cities built in haste,
As richer grander plans appeared,
And then one day they disappeared.

The blocks of cement and concrete halls,
And shining glass of buildings' walls,
And maps that forged the city's climb
Were buried by the sands of time.

Upon the sands a village lay,
Among the fields of wheat and hay,
And shady trees and shining streams,
And quiet roads and simple dreams.

As time went by the village grew . . . .

Sheila & Ron Stewart

In the whole scheme of things, earth is a fairly small dot in the universe.

EARTH

On a planet deep in space
A future city stands,
Where ships are launched to visit stars
And other distant lands.

The planet earth lies on a map,
A tiny criss-crossed dot,
Its unimportance overlooked
While other worlds are sought.

The captains guide their spaceships past
At twice the speed of light,
And wonder at the tiny blip
Recorded in their flight.

Too small and insignificant
For anyone to care,
It isn't worth the time to stop
To see if life is there.

Most of us have waited in a traffic jam and wondered why everyone has decided to drive at the same time . . . which for some strange reason usually coincides with the time that we have decided to drive.

RUSH HOUR

Rush hour traffic slowly crawls
Between the curbs and concrete walls
Of city streets and freeway lanes
And ramps and drives and other mains.

A traffic jam somewhere ahead
Has forced the cars to stop like dead
Metal bodies on the cement,
Their freedom and their progress spent.

The traffic moves and in a while
The cars have crept another mile,
And like a train that's twelve miles long,
Each seems to pull the next along.

Twice a day they all converge,
And stop and start and turn and merge,
And race and rev and sit and wait,
And hurry only to be late.

Eventually the traffic thins,
And hours after it begins,
The honking and the howling cease,
And cities lie in semi peace.

But soon the flow begins to build,
As routes to work or home are filled,
And past the curbs and concrete walls,
The rushing traffic slowly crawls.

Sometimes we are forced to drive through slums. Sometimes we choose to drive through them. Whatever our reason, we always seem to be in a hurry to leave them.

SLUMS

The cars go by and people stare
At slums they can't accept are there.
They shake their heads in disbelief,
And turn away to hide the grief
They feel for those whose dreams are gone,
Then take their dreams and move along.

They drive to where the grass is green,
Where they can still fulfill a dream,
Where money helps them to forget
The pain of poverty, and yet
A part of them cannot be free
From thoughts of guilt and sympathy.

The picture lingers in their minds,
Reminding them that other kinds
Of life exist they try to hide
When consciences can't face the side
Of life where pleasure seldom comes,
And hopes and dreams are lost in slums.

Ghost towns are lonely places. They were once happy and bustling, but most are now just sad and empty. We try to envision how they once were, but in the end we come back to the reality, and the destruction, and the greed, and the waste . . . .

GHOST TOWNS

A ghost town rests beneath the cliffs,
Its empty buildings strewn in drifts
Along old roads curved up to mines,
Left long ago for better times.

The streets that carried dreams of gold
Now carry ghosts and stories told
Of legends that once walked the town,
All boarded up and broken down.

Ghosts and tourists come to see
The town and how it used to be,
And search the streets and wonder why
A place like this should have to die.

A monument amid the waste
Describes the greatness of the place,
While all around, the ruins stand,
A much better monument to man.

Somewhere on some other land,
Some other mine is being planned,
Some other town is being built,
Some other mountain being killed.

Some other hills will be replaced
By man made hills of mining waste,
And when the mines have stripped them bare,
A ghost town will be all that's there.

A monument will mark the place,
Describing greatness in the waste,
While all around, the ruins will stand,
A much better monument to man.

Sheila & Ron Stewart

Flying, to most people, is just a way to get from one place to another, but for some of us it can be a little more stressful.

FEAR OF FLYING

A knot begins to close my throat,
I feel my stomach churn and rise,
I clench my hands and twist my coat,
And blink the dryness from my eyes.

While others pass and flaunt their calm,
And stroll and read and yawn and talk,
I reassure my sweaty palms,
And knees that buckle when I walk.

I grip the arms on either side,
And push my back into the seat,
And clench my lips and try to hide
My frightened heart's unsteady beat.

The plane streaks down the line of cement,
And climbs and shakes into the sky,
And joins my nerves as if it meant
To share the fear I have to fly.

There are two poems about TIME. One version signifies the end of the day . . .

TIME

Silhouettes against the sky
Appear and change and multiply,
And form a thousand brilliant frames
Of pictures in the sun's last flames,
As shadows play with evening's light
And daylight enters into night.

The sunset lingers in the west
And lulls the day to tranquil rest,
While in the east a darkness spreads
To north and south, and overhead
A half light brings to life the stars
And lights on streets and passing cars.

The colors change and slowly fade
Into the early evening's shade,
Where shadowed images of night
Dim remaining strands of light,
As sunset slowly slips away
And time completes another day.

*The other version of TIME signifies
the beginning of a new day . . .*

TIME

Silhouettes against the sky
Appear and change and multiply,
And form a thousand blackened frames
Of pictures in the sun's first flames,
As shadows play with morning light
And time completes another night.

The darkness lingers in the west
As night enjoys a final rest,
While in the east the blue sky spreads
To north and south, and overhead
A half light tries to drown the stars
And lights on streets and passing cars.

The black shapes fade and move away,
Replaced by colors of the day
That form new pictures in the light
And signify the end of night,
As darkness slowly slips away
And time begins another day.

There are many kinds of workers. Some do the work while others somehow manage to get out of doing the work. Some pitch in and help while others sit back and watch. And then there are the delegators....

WORK

There is no task that is too great,
No job that can't be done,
No peak that can't be conquered,
No fight that can't be won.

Each burden is a load of love,
Each challenge just a goal,
Each pain a simple price to pay
As we fulfill our role.

A mountain is a simple hill,
An ocean just a pond,
A desert just a grain of sand
For us to travel on.

Our work is such an easy chore,
There's really nothing to it,
The hardest job is finding
Someone else to do it.

    We don't always get rewards when we expect to get them . . . and we don't always get rewards in the way we expect to get them.

REWARDS

It's strange
How one day I can conquer the world
And the next I can't get out of bed,
How one day everything goes right,
And then I just can't get ahead.

Some days I work but can't succeed
At anything I try,
Then suddenly I reap rewards
But can't remember why.

They never seem to come at once
Or when I should expect,
I sometimes wonder why I work
If there is no affect.

But then I look around and see
Rewards that I have earned,
And I think of the experience
And all that I have learned.

That's when I know that work comes first
Before I get rewards,
And that I sometimes have to wait
For gifts my work affords.

So I will try to persevere
With patience for a while,
And I will try to do my best
And do it with a smile.

And the next time I am given
Rewards I haven't earned,
I'll think of all the other times
I worked and only learned.

And the next time that I conquer
The world and all within,
I will pause and realize
That I can't always win.

Whether it is with a family member, a good friend, a first love or a love of many years, holding hands gives us one of life's simplest and easiest to obtain feelings of closeness and security.

HOLDING YOUR HAND

I like holding your hand.
I like the touch of your fingers
As they wrap around mine,
And the closeness and friendship
And interests we find.

I like holding your hand.
I like the walks and the laughter
And the way that you care,
And the fun and adventures
And dreams that we share.

I like holding your hand.
I like the joy and the happiness
Found in your grasp,
And the love and affection
And feelings that last.

It would be difficult to find an emotion that will take us as high or as low, and that is as impulsive, unpredictable, uncertain, confusing, rewarding, and fickle as love.

LOVE IS FICKLE

One day we get it,
The next day we don't,
One day we give it,
The next day we won't.
It's nice when it comes,
And sad when it leaves,
When a new love is found,
Or an old love still grieves.

Sometimes we keep it,
We have it for life,
For one that we love,
A husband, a wife,
A sweetheart, a friend,
A sister, a brother,
Some always love us,
A father, a mother.

If we get love to stay,
As love often does,
Our love for others,
And their love for us,
It's the most precious gift
That any can give,
For love will stay with us
As long as we live.

Sheila & Ron Stewart

Happiness is so easy to find, it's surprising we don't have more of it.

HAPPINESS

Happiness is just a gift
We get to hold a while,
It's sometimes found in work or play,
Or simply as a smile.

It comes with friends and acts of love,
Or generosity,
Or selfless deeds, or sharing with
The others that we see.

It never can be bought or sold,
But always can be found,
If we just take the time to look,
For it is all around.

It is such a valued gift,
We try to keep, and yet,
The more of it we give away,
The more we seem to get.

Childhoods with families and friends, and adventures and dreams, are often the happiest and most memorable years of our lives.

MEMORIES OF LONG LONG AGO

Sometimes I think of my childhood,
And memories of long long ago,
I remember the people and places,
And faces that I used to know.

I remember the small country village
Where children all gathered to play,
And the roads through the maples and pine trees
Where I travelled to school every day.

I remember the wheat fields and pastures,
And forests and rivers and streams,
Where as cowboys and pirates and explorers,
We played our adventures and dreams.

Sometimes my memories sadden
When I think that they'll never come true,

That there'll be no more cowboys and pirates,
And adventures, and exploring to do.

There'll be no more play in the village,
Or walks up the old country road,
No more hide and go seek in the meadow
After the wheat has been mown.

The places I see in my memories,
Like words to my old nursery rhymes,
Are changed or gone or forgotten,
Or blurred by the passage of time.

But then, when I think of my childhood
And memories and pictures, I find
That although some places are blurry,
The people are clear in my mind.

Children still play in the village
And forests and meadows and streams,
And as cowboys and pirates and explorers,
Play out their adventures and dreams.

They see new friendly faces
Of people and places they know,
As they gather their dreams for the future,
And their memories of long long ago.

Christmas takes on different messages and meanings at different times in our lives, but we will never again experience the feelings of joy and anticipation that we had when we were children.

DREAMS OF CHRISTMAS

I listen to the Christmas songs
I heard so long ago,
And dream of bells and Christmas trees,
And sleighing in the snow.

I dream of gifts on Christmas day,
Of trains and drums and horns,
And of the joy and innocence
Of waking Christmas morn.

I dream the dreams that children dream,
And wish that I could see,
The Christmases I'm having now
The way they used to be.

Sheila & Ron Stewart

It is very easy to fall in love. Most of us do it lots of times. The difficult part is . . . .

FALLING IN LOVE

It wasn't hard to fall in love,
I fell time after time,
With almost any girl who smiled,
Just wanting to be kind.

But each time that I fell, I found
Love wasn't meant to be,
Although I fell in love,
They never fell in love with me.

But then one day I fell in love,
A girl I hardly knew,
Although I thought she'd laugh, she said,
I think I love you too.

I still fall in love from time to time,
It's still not hard to do,
But always with that girl who said,
I think I love you too.

Sometimes we forget how our lives are intertwined with so many other lives, and how their lives are intertwined with ours.

We are all much, much more than we think we are.

ME

I am more than I appear
When first you look at me,
I am more than just a person,
I am more than only me,

I'm part of you,
I'm part of everyone I know,
Do I not affect their lives,
Do I not help them grow.

I'm part of everything around me,
All I touch and see,
And everything around me
Is also part of me.

I am more than only flesh,
I'm more than what you see,
I am happiness for others,
They are happiness for me.

Oh, sometimes I think about
Being only me,
Not being part of others,
Or their being part of me.

But life would not be half the fun
Just doing as I felt,
I get much more from you
Than I could ever give myself.

I also have a lot to give
To others, so you see,
I am more than I appear,
I'm much much more than me.

Sheila & Ron Stewart

   Usually we know what we are doing and where we are going, but there are those days . . . .

CONFUSION

I just don't know.
I thought I did, but I don't.
I was going to do what I intended to do,
But I probably won't.

I set a course then change my mind,
And go the other way,
I never go the way I should,
In spite of what I say.

One day it seems so clear,
I know just what to do,
But then the next I turn to something
Altogether new.

I feel so sure of what to do,
But then I have a doubt,
I just can't seem to understand
What life is all about.

I know what's good and right and wrong,
I can give advice to you,
But when I have to guide myself,
I don't know what to do.

What made sense the other day
No longer will apply,
It seemed to be the thing to do,
But now I wonder why.

So if I appear to go through life
Not knowing what I'm doing,
It's probably because I don't,
Life's sometimes too confusing.

Good times are not difficult to find, but we sometimes have to search for them.

GOOD TIMES

He's looking for the good times,
He knows they must be here,
He sees that others have them
Whenever they are near.

He waits for other people
To bring him happiness,
And share the secret of their joy,
And good times they possess.

He watches dedication
And envies all they've learned,
And wonders why he cannot have
The good times they have earned.

He stares from isolation
At enjoyment all around,
And despises fellow citizens
For good times they have found.

Sometimes in anger God is blamed,
He cries, do you not care,
Why won't you give me happiness
And good times others share.

He waits for good times all his life,
He looks but doesn't see
That he must work and share and give,
Good times are seldom free.

We all know someone who consistently has a positive attitude, and always manages to remain cheerful, even in troubled times.

THE ROAD OF LIFE

For some the road of life looks smooth
Without a hill to climb,
And with each journey, happiness
Is all they seem to find.

They somehow always find a way
To win life's race of nerves,
And climb its hills and take its bumps,
And straighten out its curves.

They have learned to give and take
Life's kindness with its wrath,
And they adjust and do their best
To follow in its path.

For them, life's trip will be too short,
They'll wish they had more time
To do the many wondrous things
Their voyage lets them find.

And as they lay their bodies down,
And think of what they've done,
And reflect on their accomplishments,
And all that they have won,

Their prize will be fulfillment,
Their trophy, happiness,
Their joy, their friends and family
They shared their journey with.

And as they take one final look
Behind them, they will see
Their life was filled with even more
Than it appeared to be.

Sheila & Ron Stewart

Is there anything more miraculous and welcome than rain.

RAIN

The rain drifts down and hangs in trees,
Or swirls and dances in a breeze,
That spreads it in a million jewels
Of glistened rings in streams and pools.

The droplets cling to crackled leaves,
And shrivelled blossoms in their sheaves,
And burning grass and withered crops,
Unfolding to its welcomed drops.

The torrents flood the thirsty earth,
Where seeds and cones and buds give birth
To newborn trees and shrubs and flowers,
Rising to the falling showers.

Gray coats of dust are washed away,
And in their place a misty spray
Of green reflections in the sun
Announce at last the rain is done.

Sheila & Ron Stewart

There really isn't anything more miraculous and welcome than rain . . . but not when it is nine inches of rain accompanied by hundred mile per hour winds . . .

THE WILD WIND AND RAGING RAIN

Sometime in the night they came,
The wild wind and raging rain.
They blew in from the south and east,
And long before their blowing ceased,
They levelled steel and bricks and beams,
And roofs and walls and hopes and dreams.

They blew, then bent, then broke the trees,
They forced the wheat fields to their knees,
They fed the floods that swept away
The roads and bridges in their way,
They raged and howled until the dawn,
Then blew their last and they were gone.

No one knows just where they went,
If they still live or if they're spent,
But each time that a light wind blows
From south and east, and lightning glows,
And raindrops fall along the lake,
And stir the waves left in their wake,
In memories they come again,
The wild wind and raging rain.

To people who live in the area, The Salt River Canyon in Eastern Arizona is just a drive. To others who are not used to deep canyons, it can be a little frightening. No matter how we see it, it is a beautiful place.

THE CANYON

The road abruptly bends and falls
And cuts into the canyon's walls
That hold it high along the cliffs
Above a frightening abyss.

It plunges down and disappears
And leaves us hanging with our fears,
As empty space beyond the curves
Begins to pull on fraying nerves.

We anxiously approach the edge
And peer beyond a creviced ledge
Where pieces thunder far below
Into the canyon's river's flow.

Clinging to its jagged face,
We twist and drop toward the base,
Until the river where we forge
Across the bottom of the gorge.

We watch the road's thin ribbon thread
Up through a pass high overhead,
And filled with awe we cannot hide,
Begin to climb the other side.

There are few creations of nature as beautiful and refreshing as a clear mountain stream, and few creations of man as sad and unattractive as a dry river bed after all its water has been diverted for other uses.

THE STREAM

Somewhere under canyon walls,
Among the trees and water falls,
A tiny stream begins to flow
Toward the desert far below.

It laughs and sparkles as it flows
Among the rocks, and slowly grows
Until a mighty river drifts
Between the rocky canyon cliffs.

It cuts and curves through pasture lands
Into the thirsty desert sands,
And fills the lakes and feeds canals,
And dry deserted desert wells.

Then somewhere far from canyon walls,
And mountain trees and water falls,
Where once the mighty river turned,
A river bed lies cracked and burned.

A tiny stream, its sparkle gone,
No water left to carry on,
Cries and trickles into tears,
Before it slowly disappears.

The desert can be a barren place, but many have made it their home, and wouldn't trade it for anything else.

THE BARREN LAND

The desert is a barren land
That tries to take you by the hand
And lead you from the travelled path
Where in the wilderness at last
You'll find the peacefulness you sought
A peacefulness that can't be bought
In any store or other place
Where you are just another face.

But in the desert you will find
The cost is high for peace of mind,
And many say that only fools
Would dare to go where nature rules,

Where death awaits at every turn
And desert heat begins to burn
Into your fears and on your own
You stand and fight or die alone.

The choice is yours to live or die,
Succeed or fail, and wonder why,
Or know that even fools may find
A place that offers peace of mind.
So let the desert take its price
Of pain and work and sacrifice,
And sweat and blood, for if you can,
It will let you be a man.

You won't be like other men
Who only know peace now and then,
Who stand in crowds and wait in line
To try to buy their peace of mind.
Your peace of mind will be within
If you can make the fight and win
Against the barren desert land
When it takes you by the hand.

The desert can be frightening, and at times so peaceful we wish we had spent more time there.

DESERT DRIVE

The road twists in a long curved thread
As it unfolds for miles ahead,
While in the mirror the road behind
Disappears into another time.

We blink our eyes to stay awake,
And sing a song and love and hate
The beauty of the desert floor,
As far as we can see and more.

It's frightening to us and yet,
When we're through it we'll regret
That we did not stop to share
The peacefulness it offered there.

dogs & clouds & love & life

The drive goes on forever
across the desert.
Mountains that seemed so near
are far away.
We finally catch them,
only to have them disappear
slowly behind us,
and be replaced
by other mountains.
There are no clouds
to break the monotony of the sun,
and the morning warmth
slowly gives way to the heat.
It's quiet.
There are no sounds,
except the whirl of the tires
and the silence of the wind
as they try to lull us to sleep.
There are no trees or rivers,
only cactus,
and sand,
and sagebrush,
and tumbleweeds,
and mesquite,
or whatever those dry bushes are
that cover the earth
and stop the desert from blowing away.

Sheila & Ron Stewart

Mountains are like many of the other climbs and struggles we face in life. From a distance they don't appear so insurmountable. But when we're in them . . . .

MOUNTAINS

In the distance the mountains lie,
A thin gray line against the sky,
All veiled in misty morning shrouds,
And halloed by the fluffy clouds.

As we near, the mountains grow,
The shrouds of mist now fall below
Its peaks, and clouds that filled the sky
Drift part way up the mountain's side.

The road begins to curve and rise,
And now we feel the mountain's size,
As high above stretch shadowed lines
Of rocks and cliffs and scraggy pines.

High above them, capped with snow,
Surrounded by the morning's glow,
The mountain's summits catch the sun
As they awaken one by one.

We climb its walls to dizzying heights,
Where roads above twist out of sight,
And with each conquered hill we seek
The last, but find another peak.

New peaks eclipse the ones just climbed,
As roads we travelled fall behind,
We pass through clouds one after one,
And rise into the noon day sun.

Somewhere, not knowing when, we find
There are no higher peaks to climb,
Our descent begins cloud after cloud
Toward the misty evening shroud.

We drive toward the night until
There are no cliffs and peaks and hills,
And far behind the mountains lie,
A thin gray line against the sky.

Railway tracks are always there. We cross them, or we follow them, or they follow us. And then they disappear. We don't know where they go, and we are often left wondering if they ever come to an end.

RAILWAY TRACKS

We lose them in the terminals
Beneath the city's core,
Or deep inside a mountain
Through a tunnel's darkened door.

They hide in man made canyons
Through the nation's hustled heart,
And blackened underpasses
Where they hold the world apart.

They lie in quiet valleys,
And the only way we know
Is by a hanging trail of smoke
Or engine's whistle's blow.

They disappear into the night,
Or fade around a bend,
We never see the tracks begin,
And never see them end.

Trains often remind older people of their youth, and there is sometimes a happy nostalgia, mixed with a certain amount of sadness, when they talk about them.

THE OLD MAN AND THE TRAIN

The old man talked of younger days,
And coal black smoke through morning haze,
And waking from a half sleep dream
To click of wheels and hiss of steam.

He reminisced about the trains,
And engineers and engines' names,
And lonesome whistles in the night,
And shadows from an engine's light.

He searched his memories from the past,
And tried to make the visions last,
Then bowed his head to hide the tears
Of pain of missing younger years.

Truck drivers have a need for independence and freedom that is difficult to understand . . . unless you happen to be a truck driver.

TRUCK DRIVERS

The big trucks rumble through the night
As their drivers guide their flight
On lonely blackened empty roads
That whine beneath the heavy loads.

The drivers search the beams of light
Spread out before them in the night,
And look for other trucks to greet,
And wave to friends they'll never meet.

Half hypnotized they follow lines
And posts and rails and highway signs,
And open eyes that want to close,
And wonder at the life they chose.

They'll vow they're giving up the road,
Then ask to take another load,
And drive and talk and swear and sing,
And live the life their big trucks bring.

Hitchhiking is all right, as long as we're not in a hurry to go anywhere, and it doesn't rain, and somebody is willing to give us a ride, and we don't get picked up by the police, and we don't get mugged, and we don't get run over, and . . . .

THE HITCHHIKER

The hitchhiker's thumb is in the air,
He smiles as we drive by,
He knows that we will pick him up,
He keeps his spirits high.

As time goes by his spirits change,
He doesn't try to hide
Indignance that he feels because
He doesn't have a ride.

He waves his hand and jerks his arm,
Each driver feels his glare.
He makes us feel a taste of guilt
To pass him standing there.

He snarls and spits and swears at us,
And curses everyone
Who leaves him waiting by the road,
He gestures with his thumb.

Now he lies beside the road,
His head rests in the grass,
His eyes are closed in peaceful sleep
As cars go speeding past.

A little sign stands near the road,
His destination there,
Telling where he wants to go,
If anybody cares.

Limericks can be a lot of fun, and are some of the easiest and most enjoyable poems to create.

dogs & clouds & love & life

**A debonair man from Encanto,
Said, I can dance any dance that I want to.
He was smooth on the floor,
But became such a bore,
That the ladies all told him, no thank you.**

Sheila & Ron Stewart

**A vain lady, quite slender, renowned,
Decided to lose a few pounds.
She ate diet sized bites
From morning 'till night,
And instead gained forty-eight pounds.**

HARRY

A fickle young lady we knew,
Found a handsome new gentleman who
Had muscles on muscles
And blonde hair of tussles,
And her beau didn't know what to do.

Oh, how does a broken heart share
A love with a new love affair,
That's attractive and caring
And graceful and daring
And filled with flirtation and flair.

He continued to love her of course,
For sharing her love could be worse,
Her heart was enamored
By good nature and manners,
And stolen by Harry the horse.

Sheila & Ron Stewart

A racer who bragged he was fast,
And who claimed many wins in the past,
Stopped to gloat at the gate,
And started out late,
And instead of a win, finished last.

A robber just let out on bail,
Planned a robbery with every detail,
Until a bank teller asked
Why he'd not worn a mask,
He said, "Oops,"
And went straight back to jail.

Sheila & Ron Stewart

A golfer named Shamus McDuff,
Bragged that golfing's not tough.
His swings were all strong
And his drives were all long,
But he hit every ball in the rough.

**A golfer we called Dead Eye Dan,
Always knew where his golf ball would land.
His drives all took flight
To the left or the right,
Or the lake or the rough or the sand.**

Golf is a really easy game. All we have to do is put that little ball into that little hole . . .

THE PUTT

He lined the ball up with his eye,
A simple putt to make,
One easy stroke into the cup
Was all that it would take.

With confidence his putter moved,
The ball rolled straight and true,
It glided o'er the grassy green
As to the hole it flew.

He knew not how it missed the cup,
Perhaps a blade of grass
Had caused the ball to change its course
And go on speeding past.

His second putt was lined up now,
Toward the cup it rolled,
He saw it take a solid line,
He knew he had it holed.

It must have been a gust of wind,
Or mark from someone's shoe,
Or dip or break or someone coughed,
That sent the ball askew.

He watched his third putt long and hard,
He studied all the breaks,
He squeezed his putter tight until
His hands began to ache.

The ball broke left, then right, then left,
Then ringed the orifice,
It didn't matter anymore,
He knew the putt would miss.

His fourth putt didn't take as long,
No worry or mistake,
He drove the golf ball off the green,
Into a distant lake.

THE PUTT is from:
500 MORE ALL TIME FUNNIEST GOLF JOKES, STORIES AND FAIRWAY WISDOM

There are two slightly different poems about woman. The longer version was written first. The shorter version was written in an effort to better express the mysteries of women. It didn't work. They are still a mystery, but a wonderful and exciting mystery.

WOMAN

A woman is filled with laughter and pain,
And emotions and logic no man can explain.

She is gossip and caring and sorrow and glee,
And a need to be held and a need to be free.

She is goodness and virtue of heavenly choirs,
And devilish mischief and wicked desires.

She is innocence and wisdom and deep mystery,
And excitement and all things a woman should be.

WOMAN

A woman is made up
Of sweetness and pain,
And emotions and logic
No man can explain.

She is love and indifference
And passion and glee,
And a need to be held
And a need to be free.

She is goodness and virtue
Of heavenly choirs,
And devilish mischief
And wicked desires.

She is filled with youth's innocence
And wisdom of years,
And gossip and caring
And laughter and tears.

She is predictable and obvious
And deep mystery,
And excitement
And all things a woman should be.

Sheila & Ron Stewart

We may not always understand why men do some of the things they do. We just know that when they become fathers, they change and play a special and invaluable role in their childrens' lives.

FATHERS

Fathers are a special batch
Of men who burp and cuss and scratch,
And joke and yawn and yell and spit,
And play in dirt and grease and grit.

They teach us how to throw a ball,
And cheer and lift us when we fall,
And laugh and sing our favorite song,
And let us know what's right or wrong.

They hug and care and guide and give,
And show us how to love and live.

Sheila & Ron Stewart

Like fathers and mothers, grandparents play a very special and invaluable role in their grandchildrens' lives, and have a bond that can never be broken . . .

Well, almost never broken . . .

GRANDPARENTS

The worry and the sleepless nights,
The burden through the years,
The cost and care of raising them
Through good times and through tears,
They are a joy to love and hold,
For when the visit's done,
We give them to their Moms and Dads,
Being Grandparents sure is fun.

Husbands and fathers are the same, and yet they are different . . .

Fathers enjoy playing ball, and rolling on the floor, and singing, and teaching, and having fun, and . . .

Husbands enjoy fixing things . . .

FIXING THINGS

He pressed his ear toward the squeaks,
And gurgled hissing fumes,
His wife watched, then politely asked,
Will it be working soon . . . ?

He grabbed a driver and a wrench,
I'm thinking, he replied,
And while he checked some clanking clues,
It coughed and wheezed and died.

Have you looked at the instruction book,
She asked, it could assist,
And help you see just what went wrong,
Or find something you missed.

I don't need instruction books,
He smirked a knowledged smirk,
They waste my time and interfere,
And interrupt my work.

Are you sure of what you're doing,
She soothed with words polite,
She watched him wield a five pound sledge,
And hoped she wasn't right.

I'm sure, he said, although
He'd never serviced it before,
He was certain he could fix it,
Once he found a service door.

How long, his wife asked once again,
Before you make it work.
He turned a screw, a cover flew,
It opened with a jerk.

How much longer would he be,
He shouldn't be too long,
If he could find a starter switch,
So he could turn it on.

Aha, he suddenly exclaimed,
I see the problem now,
That thing that holds that other thing,
Got loose and moved somehow.

He put it back together,
A miracle, it starts,
He wouldn't have believed it
When he had it all apart.

I have it fixed, he said with pride,
Surprised at what he'd done,
His wife smiled sweetly in support,
And prayed that he had won.

He gathered up his many tools,
His service at an end,
No sooner were they put away,
It hissed and clanked again.

They watched it shake across the floor,
I'll call someone, she pled,
He gave a royal service wave
To calm her growing dread.

His face took a determined look,
His jaw a grimaced grin,
He strapped his tool belt to his side,
And bravely went back in.

He laid out wrenches, saws and drills,
And files and rules and slides,
And nuts and bolts and chucks and keys,
And amps and voltage guides.

His wife watched as he sorted out
The clinks and clanks and clamor,
He shook his head, then nodding, said,
I think I'll need a larger hammer.

Success can be measured in many ways. Sometimes it is earned by dedication, desire, and hard work, but mostly it is obtained by just being satisfied with who we are. If we are happy with our lives while making others around us happy, we are already a success.

SUCCESS

Success is often measured by
      possessions that are owned,
Or wealth, or deeds, or power,
      or how well a name is known.

We stand in awe and wish that we
      could be what they became,
And share their recognition
      and respect and wealth and fame.

But how much would we really give
      to be what they've become,
Would we be prepared to do
      the things that they have done.

Would we be prepared to spend
      the hours they have spent,
And face the work and sacrifice
      and struggle it has meant.

Would we dedicate our lives
      to helping someone else,
And share the time and energy
      we once kept for ourselves.

Would we act responsibly
      if power came our way,
Knowing we affected lives
      of others every day.

And if our names were up in lights
      for all the world to see,
Could we let the public probe
      our anonymity.

Could a name that's up in lights
      for all the world to see,
Mean more than what a name is worth
      to friends and family.

Could a deed that's done for gain
      or notoriety,
Ever mean as much as deeds
      of love done quietly.

Could admiration and respect
      for power fame or wealth,
Equal honor and respect
      that we have for ourselves.

Could all those measurements of man
      really bring success,
Unless they brought us peace of mind,
      and love and happiness.

* * * * *

acadiascale.com

**Acadia Scale Press books
may be purchased at
amazon.com
barnes&noble.com
Barnes & Noble Book Stores
Borders Book Stores
borders.com
and other book and gift stores.**

**Most stores will be happy to order books
if they do not have a copy in stock.
Stores may order through
INGRAM BOOK COMPANY
and other book distributors.**